# How to use this book



## I AM ANGRY

I AM ANGRY BECAUSE _______________________________

MY HEAD FEELS _______________________________

MY STOMACH FEELS _______________________________

WHAT I WANT TO SCREAM OUT LOUD _______________________________

_______________________________

_______________________________



I will count to 10 slowly, now

1 2 3 4 5 6 7 8 9 10



I can see _______________

I can hear _______________

I can touch _______________

Take five deep breaths

1 2 3 4 5

I will shrink my anger down

## I AM CALMER





Colour the calming picture, and follow the last exercises

# I AM ANGRY

I AM ANGRY BECAUSE ______________________________

MY HEAD FEELS ______________________________

MY STOMACH FEELS ______________________________

WHAT I WANT TO SCREAM OUT LOUD ______________________________

______________________________

______________________________

*I will count to 10 slowly, now*

1 2 3 4 5 6 7 8 9 10

I can see ______________

I can hear ______________

I can touch ______________

*Take five deep breaths*

1 2 3 4 5

*I will shrink my anger down*

# I AM CALMER

Scribble out my scream out loud words
then write calmly how I feel about the situation

_______________________________

_______________________________

# I AM CALM

Share how I feel with someone

# I AM ANGRY

I AM ANGRY BECAUSE _________________________________

MY HEAD FEELS _________________________________

MY STOMACH FEELS _________________________________

WHAT I WANT TO SCREAM OUT LOUD _________________________________

_________________________________

_________________________________

*I will count to 10 slowly, now*

1 2 3 4 5 6 7 8 9 10

I can see _________________________________

I can hear _________________________________

I can touch _________________________________

*Take five deep breaths*

1 2 3 4 5

*I will shrink my anger down*

# I AM CALMER

Scribble out my scream out loud words
then write calmly how I feel about the situation



I AM CALM



Share how I feel with someone

# I AM ANGRY

I AM ANGRY BECAUSE _______________________________________

MY HEAD FEELS _________________________________

MY STOMACH FEELS ___________________________

WHAT I WANT TO SCREAM OUT LOUD _________________________

_______________________________________________

_______________________________________________

*I will count to 10 slowly, now*

1 2 3 4 5 6 7 8 9 10

*I can see* _______________

*I can hear* _______________

*I can touch* _______________

*Take five deep breaths*

1 2 3 4 5

*I will shrink my anger down*

# I AM CALMER

*Scribble out my scream out loud words
then write calmly how I feel about the situation*

________________________________________

________________________________________

# I AM CALM

*Share how I feel with someone*

# I AM ANGRY

I AM ANGRY BECAUSE ___________________________________

MY HEAD FEELS ___________________________

MY STOMACH FEELS ___________________________

WHAT I WANT TO SCREAM OUT LOUD ___________________________

___________________________________

___________________________________

*I will count to 10 slowly, now*

1 2 3 4 5 6 7 8 9 10

I can see ___________

I can hear ___________

I can touch ___________

*Take five deep breaths*

1 2 3 4 5

*I will shrink my anger down*

# I AM CALMER

Scribble out my scream out loud words
then write calmly how I feel about the situation

I AM CALM

Share how I feel with someone

# I AM ANGRY

**I AM ANGRY BECAUSE** ______________________________________________

**MY HEAD FEELS** ______________________________

**MY STOMACH FEELS** ______________________________

**WHAT I WANT TO SCREAM OUT LOUD** ______________________

______________________________________________

______________________________________________

*I will count to 10 slowly, now*

1 2 3 4 5 6 7 8 9 10

I can see ______________

I can hear ______________

I can touch ______________

*Take five deep breaths*

1 2 3 4 5

*I will shrink my anger down*

# I AM CALMER

Scribble out my scream out loud words
then write calmly how I feel about the situation

## I AM CALM

Share how I feel with someone

# I AM ANGRY

**I AM ANGRY BECAUSE** _______________________________________

**MY HEAD FEELS** _____________________________

**MY STOMACH FEELS** _______________________

**WHAT I WANT TO SCREAM OUT LOUD** _____________________

_______________________________________________

_______________________________________________

*I will count to 10 slowly, now*

1 2 3 4 5 6 7 8 9 10

*I can see* ____________

*I can hear* ____________

*I can touch* ____________

*Take five deep breaths*

1 2 3 4 5

*I will shrink my anger down*

# I AM CALMER

Scribble out my scream out loud words
then write calmly how I feel about the situation

I AM CALM

Share how I feel with someone

# I AM ANGRY

I AM ANGRY BECAUSE _______________________________________________

MY HEAD FEELS _______________________________

MY STOMACH FEELS _________________________________

WHAT I WANT TO SCREAM OUT LOUD _______________________________

_____________________________________________________________

_____________________________________________________________

*I will count to 10 slowly, now*

1 2 3 4 5 6 7 8 9 10

*I can see* _______________

*I can hear* _______________

*I can touch* _______________

*Take five deep breaths*

1 2 3 4 5

*I will shrink my anger down*

# I AM CALMER

Scribble out my scream out loud words
then write calmly how I feel about the situation

I AM CALM

Share how I feel with someone

# I AM ANGRY

I AM ANGRY BECAUSE ___________________________________________

MY HEAD FEELS _______________________________

MY STOMACH FEELS _______________________________

WHAT I WANT TO SCREAM OUT LOUD _______________________

_____________________________________________________________

_____________________________________________________________

*I will count to 10 slowly, now*

1 2 3 4 5 6 7 8 9 10

*I can see* _______________

*I can hear* _______________

*I can touch* _______________

*Take five deep breaths*

1 2 3 4 5

*I will shrink my anger down*

# I AM CALMER

Scribble out my scream out loud words
then write calmly how I feel about the situation

I AM CALM

Share how I feel with someone

# I AM ANGRY

I AM ANGRY BECAUSE ________________________________

MY HEAD FEELS ____________________________

MY STOMACH FEELS ______________________________

WHAT I WANT TO SCREAM OUT LOUD ____________________

________________________________________________

________________________________________________

*I will count to 10 slowly, now*

1 2 3 4 5 6 7 8 9 10

I can see ______________

I can hear ______________

I can touch ______________

*Take five deep breaths*

1 2 3 4 5

*I will shrink my anger down*

# I AM CALMER

*Scribble out my scream out loud words*
*then write calmly how I feel about the situation*

___________________________________

___________________________________

# I AM CALM

*Share how I feel with someone*

# I AM ANGRY

**I AM ANGRY BECAUSE** _______________________________________________

**MY HEAD FEELS** _______________________________

**MY STOMACH FEELS** _________________________________

**WHAT I WANT TO SCREAM OUT LOUD** _____________________________

_______________________________________________________________

_______________________________________________________________

*I will count to 10 slowly, now*

1 2 3 4 5 6 7 8 9 10

*I can see* _______________

*I can hear* _______________

*I can touch* _______________

*Take five deep breaths*

1 2 3 4 5

*I will shrink my anger down*

# I AM CALMER

Scribble out my scream out loud words
then write calmly how I feel about the situation

I AM CALM

Share how I feel with someone

# I AM ANGRY

I AM ANGRY BECAUSE ___________________________________

MY HEAD FEELS ___________________________

MY STOMACH FEELS ______________________________

WHAT I WANT TO SCREAM OUT LOUD ___________________________

_______________________________________________________

_______________________________________________________

*I will count to 10 slowly, now*

1 2 3 4 5 6 7 8 9 10

*I can see* ______________

*I can hear* ______________

*I can touch* ______________

*Take five deep breaths*

1 2 3 4 5

*I will shrink my anger down*

# I AM CALMER

I AM CALM

Share how I feel with someone

# I AM ANGRY

I AM ANGRY BECAUSE ______________________________________________

MY HEAD FEELS ___________________________

MY STOMACH FEELS ______________________________

WHAT I WANT TO SCREAM OUT LOUD ____________________________

______________________________________________

______________________________________________

*I will count to 10 slowly, now*

1 2 3 4 5 6 7 8 9 10

*I can see* ___________________

*I can hear* ___________________

*I can touch* ___________________

*Take five deep breaths*

1 2 3 4 5

*I will shrink my anger down*

# I AM CALMER

_Scribble out my scream out loud words_
_then write calmly how I feel about the situation_

___________________________________

___________________________________

# I AM CALM

_Share how I feel with someone_

# I AM ANGRY

I AM ANGRY BECAUSE ___________________________________

MY HEAD FEELS _______________________

MY STOMACH FEELS _________________________

WHAT I WANT TO SCREAM OUT LOUD _______________________

______________________________________________________

*I will count to 10 slowly, now*

1 2 3 4 5 6 7 8 9 10

*I can see* ______________

*I can hear* ______________

*I can touch* ______________

*Take five deep breaths*

1 2 3 4 5

*I will shrink my anger down*

# I AM CALMER

*Scribble out my scream out loud words
then write calmly how I feel about the situation*

___________________________________

___________________________________

# I AM CALM

*Share how I feel with someone*

# I AM ANGRY

**I AM ANGRY BECAUSE** _______________________________________

**MY HEAD FEELS** _______________________________

**MY STOMACH FEELS** _______________________________

**WHAT I WANT TO SCREAM OUT LOUD** _______________________

_______________________________________________________

_______________________________________________________

*I will count to 10 slowly, now*

1  2  3  4  5  6  7  8  9  10

*I can see* _______________

*I can hear* _______________

*I can touch* _______________

*Take five deep breaths*

1  2  3  4  5

*I will shrink my anger down*

# I AM CALMER

_______________________________________________

_______________________________________________

## I AM CALM

Share how I feel with someone

# I AM ANGRY

I AM ANGRY BECAUSE ___________________________________

MY HEAD FEELS ___________________________

MY STOMACH FEELS ___________________________

WHAT I WANT TO SCREAM OUT LOUD ___________________

___________________________________________________

___________________________________________________

*I will count to 10 slowly, now*

1 2 3 4 5 6 7 8 9 10

*I can see* ______________

*I can hear* ______________

*I can touch* ______________

*Take five deep breaths*

1 2 3 4 5

*I will shrink my anger down*

# I AM CALMER

Scribble out my scream out loud words
then write calmly how I feel about the situation

_____________________________________

_____________________________________

# I AM CALM

Share how I feel with someone

# I AM ANGRY

I AM ANGRY BECAUSE ___________________________________

MY HEAD FEELS ___________________________

MY STOMACH FEELS ___________________________

WHAT I WANT TO SCREAM OUT LOUD ___________________________

___________________________________________________________

___________________________________________________________

*I will count to 10 slowly, now*

1 2 3 4 5 6 7 8 9 10

*I can see* ___________

*I can hear* ___________

*I can touch* ___________

*Take five deep breaths*

1 2 3 4 5

*I will shrink my anger down*

# I AM CALMER

_Scribble out my scream out loud words
then write calmly how I feel about the situation_

______________________________________

______________________________________

# I AM CALM

_Share how I feel with someone_

# I AM ANGRY

I AM ANGRY BECAUSE _______________________________________________

MY HEAD FEELS _____________________________

MY STOMACH FEELS _______________________________

WHAT I WANT TO SCREAM OUT LOUD _______________________________

_______________________________________________________________

_______________________________________________________________

*I will count to 10 slowly, now*

1 2 3 4 5 6 7 8 9 10

*I can see* _______________

*I can hear* _______________

*I can touch* _______________

*Take five deep breaths*

1 2 3 4 5

*I will shrink my anger down*

# I AM CALMER

Scribble out my scream out loud words
then write calmly how I feel about the situation

I AM CALM

Share how I feel with someone

# I AM ANGRY

I AM ANGRY BECAUSE _______________________________________

MY HEAD FEELS _______________________________

MY STOMACH FEELS _______________________________

WHAT I WANT TO SCREAM OUT LOUD _______________________

_____________________________________________________

_____________________________________________________

*I will count to 10 slowly, now*

1   2   3   4   5   6   7   8   9   10

*I can see* _______________

*I can hear* _______________

*I can touch* _______________

*Take five deep breaths*

1   2   3   4   5

*I will shrink my anger down*

# I AM CALMER

*Scribble out my scream out loud words*
*then write calmly how I feel about the situation*

___________________________________________

___________________________________________

# I AM CALM

*Share how I feel with someone*

# I AM ANGRY

I AM ANGRY BECAUSE ___________________________________________

MY HEAD FEELS ______________________________

MY STOMACH FEELS ___________________________

WHAT I WANT TO SCREAM OUT LOUD ___________________________

_________________________________________________________

_________________________________________________________

*I will count to 10 slowly, now*

1 2 3 4 5 6 7 8 9 10

*I can see* ______________

*I can hear* ______________

*I can touch* ______________

*Take five deep breaths*

1 2 3 4 5

*I will shrink my anger down*

# I AM CALMER

Scribble out my scream out loud words
then write calmly how I feel about the situation

_______________________________________

_______________________________________

# I AM CALM

Share how I feel with someone

# I AM ANGRY

**I AM ANGRY BECAUSE** _______________________________________

**MY HEAD FEELS** _______________________________

**MY STOMACH FEELS** _______________________________

**WHAT I WANT TO SCREAM OUT LOUD** _______________________

_______________________________________________________

_______________________________________________________

*I will count to 10 slowly, now*

1 2 3 4 5 6 7 8 9 10

*I can see* _______________

*I can hear* _______________

*I can touch* _______________

*Take five deep breaths*

1 2 3 4 5

*I will shrink my anger down*

# I AM CALMER

Scribble out my scream out loud words
then write calmly how I feel about the situation

_______________________________________________

_______________________________________________

# I AM CALM

Share how I feel with someone

# I AM ANGRY

**I AM ANGRY BECAUSE** _______________________________________

**MY HEAD FEELS** _______________________________

**MY STOMACH FEELS** _______________________________

**WHAT I WANT TO SCREAM OUT LOUD** _______________________

_______________________________________________________________

_______________________________________________________________

*I will count to 10 slowly, now*

1 2 3 4 5 6 7 8 9 10

I can see _______________

I can hear _______________

I can touch _______________

*Take five deep breaths*

1 2 3 4 5

*I will shrink my anger down*

# I AM CALMER

Scribble out my scream out loud words
then write calmly how I feel about the situation

_______________________________________

_______________________________________

# I AM CALM

Share how I feel with someone

# I AM ANGRY

I AM ANGRY BECAUSE ___________________________________

MY HEAD FEELS _________________________

MY STOMACH FEELS ___________________________

WHAT I WANT TO SCREAM OUT LOUD _________________________

___________________________________________________

___________________________________________________

I will count to 10 slowly, now

1 2 3 4 5 6 7 8 9 10

I can see _______________

I can hear _______________

I can touch _______________

Take five deep breaths

1 2 3 4 5

I will shrink my anger down

# I AM CALMER

*Scribble out my scream out loud words*
*then write calmly how I feel about the situation*

___________________________________________

___________________________________________

# I AM CALM

*Share how I feel with someone*

# I AM ANGRY

I AM ANGRY BECAUSE _______________________________________

MY HEAD FEELS _____________________________

MY STOMACH FEELS _______________________________

WHAT I WANT TO SCREAM OUT LOUD _________________________

_______________________________________________________

_______________________________________________________

*I will count to 10 slowly, now*

1 2 3 4 5 6 7 8 9 10

*I can see* _______________

*I can hear* _______________

*I can touch* _______________

*Take five deep breaths*

1 2 3 4 5

*I will shrink my anger down*

# I AM CALMER

*Scribble out my scream out loud words
then write calmly how I feel about the situation*

______________________________________

______________________________________

## I AM CALM

*Share how I feel with someone*

# I AM ANGRY

I AM ANGRY BECAUSE _______________________________________

MY HEAD FEELS _______________________________

MY STOMACH FEELS _______________________________

WHAT I WANT TO SCREAM OUT LOUD _______________________

_______________________________________________________

_______________________________________________________

*I will count to 10 slowly, now*

1 2 3 4 5 6 7 8 9 10

*I can see* _______________

*I can hear* _______________

*I can touch* _______________

*Take five deep breaths*

1 2 3 4 5

*I will shrink my anger down*

# I AM CALMER

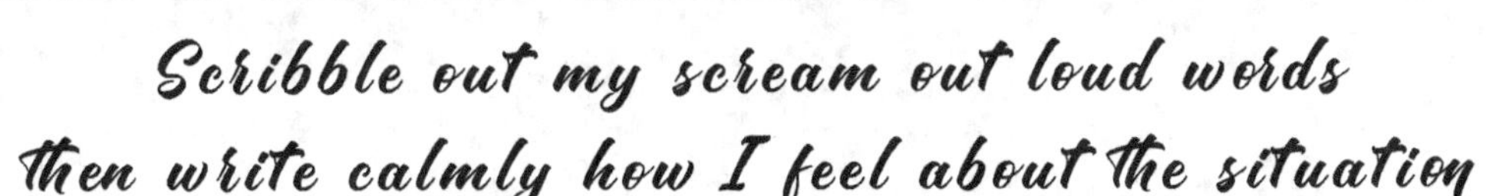

*Scribble out my scream out loud words
then write calmly how I feel about the situation*

___________________________________

___________________________________

# I AM CALM

*Share how I feel with someone*

# I AM ANGRY

I AM ANGRY BECAUSE _______________________________________________

MY HEAD FEELS _________________________________

MY STOMACH FEELS _________________________________

WHAT I WANT TO SCREAM OUT LOUD _________________________________

_______________________________________________

_______________________________________________

*I will count to 10 slowly, now*

1 2 3 4 5 6 7 8 9 10

*I can see* _________________

*I can hear* _________________

*I can touch* _________________

*Take five deep breaths*

1 2 3 4 5

*I will shrink my anger down*

# I AM CALMER

Scribble out my scream out loud words
then write calmly how I feel about the situation

I AM CALM

Share how I feel with someone